discover your spiritual gifts the network way

Resources from Bruce Bugbee

Network

Discover Your Spiritual Gifts the Network Way

What You Do Best in the Body of Christ

A NETWORK MINISTRY RESOURCE

discover your spiritual gifts
the gifts network way

4 Assessments for Determining Your Spiritual Gifts

bruce bugbee

GRAND RAPIDS, MICHIGAN 49530 USA

ZONDERVAN™

Discover Your Spiritual Gifts the Network Way
Copyright © 2005 by Bruce Bugbee and Willow Creek Community Church

Requests for information should be addressed to:
Zondervan, *Grand Rapids, Michigan 49530*

ISBN-10: 0-310-25746-8
ISBN-13: 978-0-310-25746-2

Interior design by Sharon VanLoozenoord

Printed in the United States of America

12 13 /❖ DCI/ 20 19 18 17 16 15

To *friends and kingdom builders* . . .

Tom Cramer,
a longtime personal and pastoral friend
whose gifts and passion for ministry
are infectious and life-giving

Sue Mallory,
a valued friend and fellow pioneer
whose gifts and tender boldness
have fueled a movement that is equipping
the people of God and the leaders who lead them

Now concerning spiritual gifts, I do not want you to be unaware.

—*the apostle Paul (1 Cor. 12:1)*

contents

The spiritual gifts assessments in this book will assist you in better understanding the ministry role God has created for you. You are a minister and therefore have a ministry. A significant indicator of that ministry is your spiritual gifts.

The apostle Paul tells us that we are not to be unaware of or ignorant about spiritual gifts. Certainly he means each believer should know what their own spiritual gifts are, but he is saying more. Each believer should also know what all the gifts are and how God intends them to function in the body of Christ.

These assessments will help you to identify what your spiritual gifts are and to understand how to use them. Study and share them in the context of a small group, class, or ministry team. Learn about the spiritual gifts so you can affirm others in how the Holy Spirit is distributing his grace and ministering through them.

The purpose of identifying your spiritual gifts is so you will be able to learn specifically how you can contribute as you serve on various ministry teams. God expects that you will be using your gifts in ways that complement the gifts and contributions of others.

This book also includes a bonus assessment for those who are already serving in an area of ministry. This Ministry Assessment evaluates your ministry effectiveness and will help you to identify how fruitful and fulfilled you are.

A basic description of each of the spiritual gifts and of what they contribute is included to help you as you get started (pp. 59–61).

introduction

In churches large and small, city and rural, new and old, midwest and west coast, I have heard a common frustration expressed by pastors and lay leaders: "Why do so few people serve in the church? How can we get more people involved? How can we motivate our volunteers?"

Too often volunteers respond negatively to pleas for help. "I've put in my time," they say. "Now it's someone else's turn." They view service as a requirement they must tolerate or a duty they must endure—but only for a while.

I think there is good reason for this. Trying to fill all their ministry positions, church leaders have pigeonholed and stuffed into slots anyone who was willing. Then they have wondered why they had to work so hard to motivate volunteers, to pump them up and get them to hang in there.

Scripture teaches that God has given all Christians spiritual gifts, specially endowed abilities that help them do the work of ministry enthusiastically and effectively.

Spiritual gifts are special abilities distributed by the Holy Spirit to every believer for the common good of the body of Christ.

Spiritual gifts can be discovered and most effectively used in your life when you practice three foundational principles of Scripture, servanthood, and stewardship.

Scripture provides the foundation for what the church is, how it works, who you are, and how you fit into it. Cultural and traditional views of how the church should work have often quenched the vitality and effectiveness of God's people. God's Word frees Christians to serve faithfully and fruitfully.

Servanthood has to do with our heart toward God and our attitude toward ministry. It determines the purity and sincerity of our service. Authentic devotion to serving, honoring, and worshiping Christ is essential for effective ministry. Using our spiritual gifts without love accomplishes nothing (1 Cor. 13:1–3).

Stewardship is a call to accountability. Identifying and growing in our understanding of spiritual gifts should lead to responsible stewardship. We are to know about our spiritual gifts (1 Cor. 12:1) because we will be held accountable for how we use them (1 Peter 4:10; Matt. 25:14–30).

When people serve according to their giftedness, they serve competently. They are able to bring God's power and presence to others with love and grace. It is through our spiritual gifts that we demonstrate the reality of being the body of Christ.

You also have a God-given personal style and ministry passion. Your style keeps you energized and organized with genuineness and authenticity. Your passion keeps you motivated and enthusiastic. Your gifts, style, and passion make up your Servant Profile, and you can learn more about all of them in the book *What You Do Best in the Body of Christ* (for personal and small group exploration) and through *Network* (for churches, seminars, retreats).

You are the church—Christ's body—and your presence in the church makes a difference. When you begin to serve faithfully according to God's specific will for your life, you will experience personal fruitfulness and fulfillment. And together with other faithful servants, you will shape a church that radiates the life and power of the risen Christ. In such a church, the purposes of God are fulfilled. The Word is heard. Forgiveness is given. Worship is offered. Service is rendered. Needs are met. Peace is present. Grace is granted. The lost are found.

—Bruce Bugbee
Bruce Bugbee and Associates
Network Ministries International
www.brucebugbee.com
800-588-8833

The only way to definitely know what your spiritual gifts are is through repeated affirmation from others in the body of Christ. There are no tests or surveys that can affirm your gifts as effectively as feedback from those in the church where you serve.

The assessments in this book can, however, help you identify the spiritual gifts you might have.

The following four assessments have been designed to help you do just that. They act as windows to your possible giftedness by yielding insights from your ministry, life experiences, character traits, personal convictions, and the observations of others.

Experience Assessment. There can be a correlation between ministry or life experiences and spiritual gifts. This assessment explores personal experiences that might indicate which specific gifts you are most and least likely to have. If you have not served before, then you will identify which of your behaviors most approximate the behaviors of those who have certain gifts. So as you start serving, start in those areas of ministry.

Traits Assessment. There may be a correlation between your spiritual gifts and specific character traits. This assessment seeks to suggest possible gifts by identifying those traits that best characterize your typical attitudes, feelings, and actions.

Convictions Assessment. There is often a relationship between our giftedness and our convictions. Convictions often emerge through people or events God uses in our lives to give us direction, such as role models, vows or promises we make to him, what captures our attention, and our sense of calling. This assessment examines your ministry desires or convictions for possible insights regarding your giftedness.

Observation Assessment. You may be unaware of what others appreciate about you. This assessment provides people who know you well the opportunity to make observations about you and affirm areas of possible giftedness.

The accuracy and validity of each of these assessments will vary, depending on several factors:

- Your age
- How long you have been a Christian
- Your church tradition or background
- Your experiences
- Your honesty

Some of these assessments will be easier for you to complete than others. *Respond to each according to who you really are, not who you hope to be.* Be descriptive.

Appreciate the journey you are on and be patient with your progress. Do the best you can through prayerful reflection. Enjoy!

(Note: you will find instructions and an answer sheet to guide you in each section.)

experience assessment

There is often a correlation between Christian experiences and spiritual gifts. This assessment explores personal experiences that might indicate which specific gifts you are most and least likely to have. If you have not served before, then you will identify which of your behaviors most approximate the behaviors of those who have certain gifts.

Directions:

1. Read each statement in the Experience Assessment (pp. 22–30).

2. Indicate how true of you each statement is by scoring it using the following scale:

Score		Meaning
3	=	Consistently / Definitely true
2	=	Most of the time / Usually true
1	=	Some of the time / Once in a while
0	=	Never / Not at all

3. Put your score (0, 1, 2, or 3) in the appropriately numbered box on the response sheet (p. 21).

4. *Important:*
   - Answer according to who you are, not who you would like to be or think you should be.
   - How true of you are these statements?
   - What has been your experience?
   - To what degree do these statements reflect your tendencies?

5. When you have completed the Experience Assessment, add up each column and record the total above each letter.

EXPERIENCE RESPONSE SHEET

																			134	135	136	137
1	2	3	4	5	6	7	8	9	10	11	12	13	14	15	16	17	18	19				
20	21	22	23	24	25	26	27	28	29	30	31	32	33	34	35	36	37	38				
39	40	41	42	43	44	45	46	47	48	49	50	51	52	53	54	55	56	57				
58	59	60	61	62	63	64	65	66	67	68	69	70	71	72	73	74	75	76				
77	78	79	80	81	82	83	84	85	86	87	88	89	90	91	92	93	94	95				
96	97	98	99	100	101	102	103	104	105	106	107	108	109	110	111	112	113	114				
115	116	117	118	119	120	121	122	123	124	125	126	127	128	129	130	131	132	133				
A	**B**	**C**	**D**	**E**	**F**	**G**	**H**	**I**	**J**	**K**	**L**	**M**	**N**	**O**	**P**	**Q**	**R**	**S**	**T**	**U**	**V**	**W**

TOTAL

TOP THREE

The score and its meaning:

3 = Consistently / Definitely true
2 = Most of the time / Usually true
1 = Some of the time / Once in a while
0 = Never / Not at all

Respond to the statements on pages 21–30. Transfer the top three gifts from your Experience Assessment to the Spiritual Gifts Summary on page 53.

STATEMENTS

1. I can coordinate people, tasks, and events to meet a need.

2. I enjoy working creatively with wood, cloth, paints, metal, glass, or other materials.

3. I enjoy developing and using my artistic skills (art, drama, music, photography, etc.).

4. When I see spiritual complacency, I am willing to challenge it.

5. I have confidence that God not only can, but he will.

6. I give liberally and joyfully to people in financial need or to projects requiring support.

7. I enjoy working behind the scenes to support the work of others.

8. I view my home as a safe and caring place to minister to people.

9. When it comes to my attention, I am honored to regularly pray for someone or for a concern.

10. I am motivated to set goals and influence others to achieve a vision in order to advance God's work on earth.

11. I empathize with hurting people and desire to help in their healing process.

12. I am attracted to the idea of serving in another country or an ethnic community.

13. I have spoken a timely and important prophetic word to others that I felt came to me directly from God while in prayer.

14. I have the ability to communicate the gospel with clarity and conviction.

15. I establish trust and confidence through long-term relationships.

16. I am able to communicate God's Word effectively.

17. I can readily distinguish between spiritual truth and error, good and evil.

18. I research and am persistent in my pursuit of knowing the truth.

19. Others often seek me out for advice about personal and spiritual matters.

20. I am careful, thorough, and skilled at managing details.

21. I am skilled in working with different kinds of tools.

22. I help people better understand themselves, their relationships, and God through artistic expression.

23. I enjoy reassuring and strengthening those who are discouraged.

24. I have confidence in God's continuing provision and help, even in difficult times.

25. I give more than a tithe so that kingdom work can be accomplished.

26. I enjoy doing routine tasks that support the needs of ministry.

27. I enjoy meeting new people and helping them feel welcomed.

28. I enjoy praying for long periods of time and receive leadings as to what God wants me to pray for.

29. It is quite natural for me to lead, and it is more comfortable for me to lead than not to lead.

30. I can patiently support those going through painful experiences as they are seeking stability in their lives.

31. I am willing to take an active part in starting a new church.

32. By God's revelation to me, I have been able to shed light on current realities in someone's life that helps them see God's desire for their future.

33. After I have shared the story of Jesus, people pray with me for salvation.

34. I can faithfully provide long-term emotional and spiritual support and concern for others.

35. I simply and practically explain and clarify the Word for those who are confused or just do not know.

36. I have a "sixth sense" and frequently am able to identify a person's character based on first impressions.

37. I receive information from the Spirit that I did not acquire through natural means.

38. I can often find simple, practical solutions in the midst of conflict or confusion.

39. I can clarify goals and develop strategies or plans to accomplish them.

40. I can visualize how something should be constructed before I build it.

41. I like finding new and fresh ways of communicating God's truth.

42. I give hope to others by directing them to the promises of God.

43. I have a special ability to trust God for extraordinary needs.

44. I manage my money well in order to free more of it for giving.

45. I willingly take on a variety of odd jobs around the church to meet the needs of others.

46. I genuinely believe the Lord directs strangers to me who need a sense of belonging and connection to others.

47. I am conscious of ministering to others as I pray.

48. I am usually chosen as the group's spokesperson when in discussion groups.

49. I am drawn toward people who are sometimes regarded as undeserving or beyond help.

50. I can relate to others in culturally sensitive ways.

51. I speak biblical truth in a timely and culturally sensitive way in order to strengthen, encourage, and comfort God's people.

52. I'd rather be around non-Christians more than Christians so that I can build relationships with them.

53. I enjoy giving practical support, nurture, and spiritual guidance to a group of people.

54. When I teach, people respond to my teaching with action.

55. I can see through phoniness or deceit before it is evident to others.

56. I seek certainty and truth in order to avoid superficial understandings and speculation.

57. I am surprised by how many people are unable to solve problems and seem to lack common sense.

58. I can identify and effectively use the resources needed to accomplish tasks.

59. I am good at working with my hands and enjoy doing so.

60. I regularly need to get alone to reflect and to develop my imagination.

61. I reassure those who need to take courageous action in their faith, family, or life.

62. I am unwavering in my belief that God will absolutely work in circumstances in which success cannot be guaranteed by human effort alone.

63. I choose to limit my lifestyle in order to give away a higher percentage of my income.

64. I see spiritual significance in doing practical tasks.

65. I rarely meet people I do not like and wouldn't want to see included in the life of the church.

66. I pray with confidence because I know that God works in response to prayer.

67. I set goals and direct people to effectively accomplish them.

68. I have great compassion for hurting people.

69. I view the overall picture and do not get hindered with problems along the way.

70. I have spoken to others about future events or situations that God revealed to me, and they happened as I said they would.

71. I boldly speak about salvation through Jesus Christ and see a positive response in those who are listening.

72. I can gently restore wandering believers to faith and fellowship.

73. I get frustrated when I see people's lack of biblical knowledge.

74. God shows me the difference between a demonic influence, a mental illness, and an error in truth.

75. When reading or studying Scripture, I see important biblical truths and themes that benefit others in the body of Christ.

76. I can anticipate the likely consequences of the actions of an individual or a group.

77. I like to help groups become more efficient.

78. I serve and work more behind the scenes to make things that are useful for ministry and that honor God.

79. The way I say and do things awakens the truth in others, so they say, "I have never thought of it that way."

80. I find great joy in affirming the value and worth of others.

81. When I see God's activity, I move toward it in spite of opposition or a lack of support.

82. For special projects and capital campaigns, I like to give in a way that encourages and inspires others to give generously.

83. I like to find things that need to be done and often do them without being asked.

84. For me, the greatest times of joy in the church are times of social interaction and fellowship.

85. When I hear about needy situations, I feel burdened to pray.

86. I influence others to perform to the best of their ability.

87. I look through a person's handicaps or problems to see a life that matters to God and an opportunity to serve.

88. I am culturally sensitive and comfortable with different ethnic groups.

89. I feel a compulsion to speak the words God gives me to strengthen, encourage, and comfort others.

90. I openly tell people that I am a Christian and want them to ask me about my faith.

91. There are a number of people in my life that I am personally guiding with truth, encouragement, caring, and wisdom.

92. I communicate Scripture in ways that cause others to learn and become motivated toward greater growth.

93. I receive affirmation from others concerning the reliability of my insights about them and of perceptions I have of others.

94. I have suddenly known things about others, but did not know how I knew them.

95. I give practical advice to help others through complicated situations.

96. I can visualize a coming event, anticipate potential problems, and develop strategies to meet them.

97. I am a resourceful person, able to find the best materials and tools needed to build what is needed.

98. I use various forms of the arts to draw people closer to God and his truth.

99. I like motivating others to take steps for spiritual growth.

100. I am regularly challenging others to trust God.

101. I manage my money and give to ministries that are well led and are making a difference for Christ in the lives of people.

102. I show my love for others in actions more than words.

103. I do whatever I can to make visitors and others feel they belong.

104. God gives me a peace and confidence that my prayers are being answered, even when I cannot see the results.

105. I am able to cast a vision for ministry that others want to follow and be a part of.

106. I enjoy bringing hope, joy, and comfort to people working through a crisis or chronic situation in their lives.

107. I relate to leaders who often follow me into new ministry ventures.

108. God reveals to me things others cannot see so when I speak to them they can understand his activity in their lives.

109. I love unchurched people no matter where they are on their spiritual journey.

110. I take responsibility to nurture the whole person in his or her walk with God.

111. I can present information and skills to others in ways that make it easier for them to grasp and apply them to their lives.

112. I have seen into the spiritual realm where the spirits have been revealed to me by God.

113. The truths I learn and the understandings I gain create a burden for me because of the responsibility I feel to handle the information wisely.

114. When faced with how to apply biblical truths practically in a difficult or complex situation, God reveals to me a solution.

115. I want to bring order where there is organizational chaos.

116. I have good hand-eye coordination and good dexterity.

117. I have a sense of the whole and can creatively put things together in a harmonious flow that artistically communicates a biblical truth.

118. I carefully challenge or rebuke others in order to help them grow spiritually.

119. I find it natural to believe in God for things that others see as impossible.

120. I believe I have been given an abundance of resources so that I may give more to the Lord's work.

121. When a task needs to be done, I find it difficult to say no.

122. I can make people feel at ease even in unfamiliar surroundings.

123. I see specific results in direct response to my prayers.

124. I figure out where we need to go and help others to get there.

125. I am moved with compassion and motivated to remove the sources of another's sufferings.

126. God's authority and power are manifested in the new churches and ministries I served to start.

127. I feel compelled to expose sin wherever I see it and to challenge people to repentance.

128. I'm constantly thinking of ways to bring up spiritual matters with friends who do not know God.

129. I feel responsible to help oversee and protect believers from the things that keep them from fellowship with God and one another.

130. I struggle with how to take what I have been studying and communicate only those things that will help God's people learn what they need at the moment.

131. I can sense when demonic forces are at work in a person or situation.

132. I love learning and share with those who want to learn.

133. I like to read and study the book of Proverbs for its simple and powerful truths expressed in a clear and practical way.

If you have repeatedly had any of the following experiences, indicate that with a check mark by the appropriate letter on your answer sheet.

    T. I have repeatedly seen an instant healing as I laid hands on someone and prayed.

    U. When I hear people speak in tongues, I feel the Spirit revealing his message to me, and I speak it aloud, interpreting it for the church.

    V. I have experienced the power of God within me to cast out demons, have healed the sick, and have seen his supernatural intervention in nature.

    W. I have spoken in a language I did not learn and do not understand, and someone has spoken out to interpret what I had just said.

EXPERIENCE KEY

A	Administration
B	Craftsmanship
C	Creative Communication
D	Encouragement
E	Faith
F	Giving
G	Helps
H	Hospitality
I	Intercession
J	Leadership
K	Mercy
L	Apostleship
M	Prophecy
N	Evangelism
O	Shepherding
P	Teaching
Q	Discernment
R	Word of Knowledge
S	Word of Wisdom
T	Healing
U	Interpretation
V	Miracles
W	Tongues
	Other:

traits
assessment

There may be a correlation between your spiritual gifts and specific character traits. This assessment seeks to suggest possible gifts by identifying those traits that best characterize your typical attitudes, feelings, and actions.

Directions:

1. Read each word in the word groups (pp. 34–45) and circle your response according to the scale. For example:

		Not at all	Not much	Sometimes	Most of the time	All the time
A.	Thorough	1	2	3	(4)	5
	Effective	1	(2)	3	4	5
	Responsible	1	2	3	4	(5)

2. *Important:*

- Some words appear more than once.
- Answer according to who you are, not who you would like to be or think you should be.
- How true are these words of you?
- To what degree do these words reflect you?

3. *After* you have completed the Traits Assessment, go back and total your scores for each word group. Put them onto the response sheet (p. 46) to identify your top three spiritual gifts.

4. Transfer the top three gifts from your Traits Assessment to the Spiritual Gifts Summary on page 53.

Respond to the words in each group on pages 34–45.

Total your scores *only after* you have completed all the word groups.

	Not at all	Not much	Sometimes	Most of the time	All the time
A. Thorough	1	2	3	4	5
Effective	1	2	3	4	5
Responsible	1	2	3	4	5
Organized	1	2	3	4	5
Goal-Oriented	1	2	3	4	5
Efficient	1	2	3	4	5
Objective	1	2	3	4	5

A Total =

B. Creative	1	2	3	4	5
Designer	1	2	3	4	5
Handy	1	2	3	4	5
Resourceful	1	2	3	4	5
Practical	1	2	3	4	5
Helpful	1	2	3	4	5
Builder	1	2	3	4	5

B Total =

	Not at all	Not much	Sometimes	Most of the time	All the time
C. Passionate	1	2	3	4	5
Imaginative	1	2	3	4	5
Idea-Oriented	1	2	3	4	5
Artistic	1	2	3	4	5
Creative	1	2	3	4	5
Unconventional	1	2	3	4	5
Sensitive	1	2	3	4	5

C Total =

D. Positive	1	2	3	4	5
Motivating	1	2	3	4	5
Challenging	1	2	3	4	5
Affirming	1	2	3	4	5
Reassuring	1	2	3	4	5
Supportive	1	2	3	4	5
Dependable	1	2	3	4	5

D Total =

	Not at all	Not much	Sometimes	Most of the time	All the time
E. Steady	1	2	3	4	5
Optimistic	1	2	3	4	5
Trusting	1	2	3	4	5
Assured	1	2	3	4	5
Positive	1	2	3	4	5
Inspiring	1	2	3	4	5
Confident	1	2	3	4	5

E Total =

F. Benevolent	1	2	3	4	5
Resourceful	1	2	3	4	5
Charitable	1	2	3	4	5
Disciplined	1	2	3	4	5
Stewardship-Oriented	1	2	3	4	5
Generous	1	2	3	4	5
Diligent	1	2	3	4	5

F Total =

	Not at all	Not much	Sometimes	Most of the time	All the time
G. Available	1	2	3	4	5
Willing	1	2	3	4	5
Helpful	1	2	3	4	5
Reliable	1	2	3	4	5
Loyal	1	2	3	4	5
Dependable	1	2	3	4	5
Practical	1	2	3	4	5

G Total =

H. Friendly	1	2	3	4	5
Gracious	1	2	3	4	5
Inviting	1	2	3	4	5
Trusting	1	2	3	4	5
Caring	1	2	3	4	5
Kindhearted	1	2	3	4	5
Warm	1	2	3	4	5

H Total =

	Not at all	Not much	Sometimes	Most of the time	All the time
I. Advocate	1	2	3	4	5
Caring	1	2	3	4	5
Prayerful	1	2	3	4	5
Peacemaker	1	2	3	4	5
Trustworthy	1	2	3	4	5
Burden-Bearer	1	2	3	4	5
Spiritually Sensitive	1	2	3	4	5

I Total =

J. Influential	1	2	3	4	5
Diligent	1	2	3	4	5
Visionary	1	2	3	4	5
Persuasive	1	2	3	4	5
Motivating	1	2	3	4	5
Goal-Setter	1	2	3	4	5
Respected	1	2	3	4	5

J Total =

	Not at all	Not much	Sometimes	Most of the time	All the time
K. Empathetic	1	2	3	4	5
Caring	1	2	3	4	5
Responsive	1	2	3	4	5
Kind	1	2	3	4	5
Compassionate	1	2	3	4	5
Comforting	1	2	3	4	5
Burden-Bearing	1	2	3	4	5

K Total =

L. Adventurous	1	2	3	4	5
Entrepreneurial	1	2	3	4	5
Persevering	1	2	3	4	5
Adaptable	1	2	3	4	5
Culturally Sensitive	1	2	3	4	5
Risk-Taking	1	2	3	4	5
Big Picture Person	1	2	3	4	5

L Total =

	Not at all	Not much	Sometimes	Most of the time	All the time
M.Discerning	1	2	3	4	5
Compelling	1	2	3	4	5
Uncompromising	1	2	3	4	5
Outspoken	1	2	3	4	5
Authoritative	1	2	3	4	5
Truth-Telling	1	2	3	4	5
Confronting	1	2	3	4	5

M Total =

N. Candid	1	2	3	4	5
Respected	1	2	3	4	5
Influential	1	2	3	4	5
Confident	1	2	3	4	5
Commitment-Oriented	1	2	3	4	5
Spiritually Passionate	1	2	3	4	5
Articulate	1	2	3	4	5

N Total =

	Not at all	Not much	Sometimes	Most of the time	All the time
O. Nurturing	1	2	3	4	5
Guiding	1	2	3	4	5
Influencing	1	2	3	4	5
Disciple-Making	1	2	3	4	5
Protective	1	2	3	4	5
Supportive	1	2	3	4	5
Relational	1	2	3	4	5

O Total =

	Not at all	Not much	Sometimes	Most of the time	All the time
P. Disciplined	1	2	3	4	5
Perceptive	1	2	3	4	5
Teachable	1	2	3	4	5
Authoritative	1	2	3	4	5
Practical	1	2	3	4	5
Analytical	1	2	3	4	5
Articulate	1	2	3	4	5

P Total =

	Not at all 1	Not much 2	Sometimes 3	Most of the time 4	All the time 5
Q. Perceptive	1	2	3	4	5
Insightful	1	2	3	4	5
Spiritually Sensitive	1	2	3	4	5
Intuitive	1	2	3	4	5
Decisive	1	2	3	4	5
Challenging	1	2	3	4	5
Truthful	1	2	3	4	5

Q Total =

R. Inquisitive	1	2	3	4	5
Sincere	1	2	3	4	5
Observant	1	2	3	4	5
Insightful	1	2	3	4	5
Reflective	1	2	3	4	5
Studious	1	2	3	4	5
Truthful	1	2	3	4	5

R Total =

	Not at all	Not much	Sometimes	Most of the time	All the time
S. Sensible	1	2	3	4	5
Insightful	1	2	3	4	5
Practical	1	2	3	4	5
Wise	1	2	3	4	5
Fair	1	2	3	4	5
Observant	1	2	3	4	5
Common Sense	1	2	3	4	5

S Total =

T. Compassionate	1	2	3	4	5
Healer	1	2	3	4	5
Prayerful	1	2	3	4	5
Full of Faith	1	2	3	4	5
Humble	1	2	3	4	5
Persistent	1	2	3	4	5
Obedient	1	2	3	4	5

T Total =

	Not at all 1	Not much 2	Sometimes 3	Most of the time 4	All the time 5
U. Devoted	1	2	3	4	5
Spiritually Sensitive	1	2	3	4	5
Responsible	1	2	3	4	5
Obedient	1	2	3	4	5
Discerning	1	2	3	4	5
Secure	1	2	3	4	5
Listener	1	2	3	4	5

U Total = ☐

V. Bold	1	2	3	4	5
Venturesome	1	2	3	4	5
Authoritative	1	2	3	4	5
God-Fearing	1	2	3	4	5
Convincing	1	2	3	4	5
Truth-Teller	1	2	3	4	5
Unwavering	1	2	3	4	5

V Total = ☐

	Not at all	Not much	Sometimes	Most of the time	All the time
W. Sensitive	1	2	3	4	5
Prayerful	1	2	3	4	5
Yielding	1	2	3	4	5
Trusting	1	2	3	4	5
Devoted	1	2	3	4	5
Spontaneous	1	2	3	4	5
Receptive	1	2	3	4	5

W Total =

TRAITS RESPONSE SHEET

Letter	Spiritual Gift	Total	Top 3 Gifts (1, 2, 3)
A	Administration		
B	Craftsmanship		
C	Creative Communication		
D	Encouragement		
E	Faith		
F	Giving		
G	Helps		
H	Hospitality		
I	Intercession		
J	Leadership		
K	Mercy		
L	Apostleship		
M	Prophecy		
N	Evangelism		
O	Shepherding		
P	Teaching		
Q	Discernment		
R	Word of Knowledge		
S	Word of Wisdom		
T	Healing		
U	Interpretation		
V	Miracles		
W	Tongues		

Transfer the top three gifts from your Traits Assessment to the Spiritual Gifts Summary on page 53.

convictions
assessment

There is often a relationship between our giftedness and our convictions. Convictions often emerge through people or events God uses in our lives to give us direction, such as role models, vows or promises we make to him, what captures our attention, and our sense of calling. This assessment examines your ministry desires or convictions for possible insights regarding your giftedness.

Directions:

1. While you might not be able to answer each of the questions on pages 48–49, respond as best you can to those that apply to you.

2. Take your time to think about each question. If you have not had a particular experience or event in your life, don't worry about it. These are just additional windows to your giftedness.

3. There are no right or wrong answers. Reflect carefully.

4. After you have completed pages 48–49, transfer your results to page 50 and come to a conclusion as to which gifts seem to be most evident in your Convictions Assessment.

5. Transfer the top three gifts from your Convictions Assessment to the Spiritual Gifts Summary on page 53.

You might find the list of spiritual gifts described on pages 59–61 helpful in this exercise.

CONVICTIONS ASSESSMENT

My Models

We are often attracted to and admire people with similar spiritual gifts.

List the three Christians you most admire and would want to be like. What gifts do they seem to have?

Names:	Their spiritual gifts:
1.	
2.	
3.	

My Promises

We can make a promise or vow to God that may depend on a specific gift.

In the past, I have made a vow or promise to God or agreed with God to do something. What is it?

Promise or vow:	Gifts needed:
1.	
2.	
3.	

My Attention

We have been created to solve a problem, meet a need, or serve a person.

What problems, needs, or people repeatedly catch your attention and cause you to want to change something?

Problem to solve:	Gifts needed:
•	
Need to meet:	Gifts needed:
•	
Person to serve:	Gifts needed:
•	

My Calling

Our sense of calling may indicate the presence of a related gift.

What do you feel God is calling you to do for him? What gifts would be most needed to do them?

Calling:	Gifts needed:
1.	
2.	
3.	

Transfer these responses to the next page and draw your conclusions.

Put a 1, 2, and 3 in each column alongside the spiritual gifts you identified in your Convictions Assessment on pages 48–49. Indicate your overall conclusion in the last column.

CONVICTIONS RESPONSE SHEET

	Spiritual Gift	Models	Promises	Attention	Calling	Conclusion
A	Administration					
B	Craftsmanship					
C	Creative Communication					
D	Encouragement					
E	Faith					
F	Giving					
G	Helps					
H	Hospitality					
I	Intercession					
J	Leadership					
K	Mercy					
L	Apostleship					
M	Prophecy					
N	Evangelism					
O	Shepherding					
P	Teaching					
Q	Discernment					
R	Word of Knowledge					
S	Word of Wisdom					
T	Healing					
U	Interpretation					
V	Miracles					
W	Tongues					
	Other:					

Transfer the top three gifts from your Convictions Assessment to the Spiritual Gifts Summary on page 53.

observation assessment

You may be unaware of what others appreciate about you. This assessment provides people who know you well the opportunity to make observations about you and affirm areas of possible giftedness.

Directions:

1. There are three Observation Assessment forms in the back of this book (see p. 67).

2. Cut out all three and give them to Christians who:
   - have been with you in ministry situations.
   - know you well.
   - have seen you in a variety of life situations.

3. Ask them to complete the assessment form and return it to you within a few of days. When you get the assessments back, go to the last page of each Observation Assessment (p. 5) and transfer the top three gifts by putting a 1, 2, and 3 on page 52 alongside the spiritual gifts each observer identified in you.

4. After the results of all three assessments have been entered on page 52, determine as best you can what you would conclude others are seeing in you and saying about you.

5. Put your overall conclusion in the final column on page 52 and then transfer the top three gifts from your Observation Assessment to the Spiritual Gifts Summary on page 53.

OBSERVATIONS RESPONSE SHEET

	Spiritual Gift	Observer 1	Observer 2	Observer 3	Conclusion
A	Administration				
B	Craftsmanship				
C	Creative Communication				
D	Encouragement				
E	Faith				
F	Giving				
G	Helps				
H	Hospitality				
I	Intercession				
J	Leadership				
K	Mercy				
L	Apostleship				
M	Prophecy				
N	Evangelism				
O	Shepherding				
P	Teaching				
Q	Discernment				
R	Word of Knowledge				
S	Word of Wisdom				
T	Healing				
U	Interpretation				
V	Miracles				
W	Tongues				
	Other:				

Transfer the top three gifts from your Observation Assessment to the Spiritual Gifts Summary on page 53.

your spiritual gifts summary

Use this summary to get an overview of all your assessment results. Based on the amount of times a gift has been identified and those gifts with the highest scores, make an overall determination of what you understand to be your top three spiritual gifts and indicate them in the far right column.

	Spiritual Gift	Experience	Trait	Conviction	Observation	Conclusion
A	Administration					
B	Craftsmanship					
C	Creative Communication					
D	Encouragement					
E	Faith					
F	Giving					
G	Helps					
H	Hospitality					
I	Intercession					
J	Leadership					
K	Mercy					
L	Apostleship					
M	Prophecy					
N	Evangelism					
O	Shepherding					
P	Teaching					
Q	Discernment					
R	Word of Knowledge					
S	Word of Wisdom					
T	Healing					
U	Interpretation					
V	Miracles					
W	Tongues					
	Other:					

Pursue those ministry opportunities in which you can use your top spiritual gifts to serve others.

Reassess your gifts every 12 to 24 months to further understand and clarify them.

ministry
assessment

If you are now serving in a ministry, this assessment will help indicate to what degree your service is a reflection of who God has made you to be.

Directions:

1. Read the questions on page 56 in each area.

2. Use the response sheet on page 57 to circle your answers to each set of questions.

3. When finished, add up the five scores and put the total in the box at the bottom of page 57.

4. Use the summary on page 58 to evaluate your score.

MINISTRY ASSESSMENT

Your ministry should be the natural outgrowth of who God made you to be. Answer the following key questions to determine if you are now serving in the right place. Use the response sheet on page 57.

1. Does your ministry flow out of your *giftedness*?
   - Do you have the spiritual gifts needed to fulfill your ministry responsibilities?
   - Do your ministry responsibilities stretch your gifts to their fullest potential?

2. Does your ministry reflect your *passion*?
   - What need is of ultimate importance to you?
   - Does your ministry address this need in some way?

3. Are you receiving *ministry* affirmation?
   - Are you being fruitful?
   - Can you see results?
   - Are those you're serving being encouraged and challenged?

4. Are you receiving *relational* affirmation?
   - Do your coworkers within the ministry verbally affirm your contribution?
   - Do your leaders?
   - Is there a curious silence from these people about your service?

5. Are you feeling *personal* affirmation?
   - Are you feeling fulfilled?
   - Is your self-esteem healthier?
   - Do you feel better about yourself after serving in this ministry?

Indicate your response to each of the five major areas by circling the appropriate number along each continuum as it relates to your ministry involvement.

1. Spiritual Gifts

No, not at all   Yes, very much

| 1 | 2 | 3 | 4 | 5 | 6 | 7 | 8 | 9 | 10 |

2. Ministry Passion

No, not at all   Yes, very much

| 1 | 2 | 3 | 4 | 5 | 6 | 7 | 8 | 9 | 10 |

3. Ministry Affirmation

No, not at all   Yes, very much

| 1 | 2 | 3 | 4 | 5 | 6 | 7 | 8 | 9 | 10 |

4. Relational Affirmation

No, not at all   Yes, very much

| 1 | 2 | 3 | 4 | 5 | 6 | 7 | 8 | 9 | 10 |

5. Personal Affirmation

No, not at all   Yes, very much

| 1 | 2 | 3 | 4 | 5 | 6 | 7 | 8 | 9 | 10 |

Total score and go to page 58.

MINISTRY ASSESSMENT INTERPRETATION

If your score is	Consider the following interpretation and action steps:
45–50	You are probably serving in an appropriate ministry.
38–44	You are probably in the right ministry but may need to grow or make some minor adjustments to fine-tune your serving effectiveness.
30–37	Some ministry changes are necessary. Determine what is happening or is not happening and discuss this with your ministry leaders to make appropriate changes.
30 or less	Seek counsel regarding a ministry that would be more in line with who God has made you to be. Discuss this with your ministry leaders.

You are never the wrong person.
You might be the right person in the wrong position.

Everyone is a 10 . . . *somewhere!*

spiritual gifts descriptions and contributions

Administration: The divine enablement to understand what makes an organization function, and the special ability to plan and execute procedures that accomplish the goals of the ministry. Contributes: *Efficiency.*

Apostleship: The divine ability to start and oversee the development of new churches or ministry structures. Contributes: *New Ministries.*

Craftsmanship: The divine enablement to creatively design and/or construct items to be used for ministry. Contributes: *Skills.*

Creative Communication: The divine enablement to communicate God's truth through a variety of art forms. Contributes: *Artistic Expression.*

Discernment: The divine enablement to distinguish between truth and error. It is the ability to discern the spirits, differentiating between good and evil, right and wrong. Contributes: *Clarity.*

Encouragement: The divine enablement to present truth so as to strengthen, comfort, or urge to action those who are discouraged or wavering in their faith. Contributes: *Affirmation.*

Evangelism: The divine enablement to effectively communicate the gospel to unbelievers so they respond in faith and move toward discipleship. Contributes: *The Good News.*

Faith: The divine enablement to act on God's promises with confidence and unwavering belief in God's ability to fulfill his purposes. Contributes: *Confidence.*

Giving: The divine enablement to contribute money and resources to the work of the Lord with cheerfulness and liberality. Contributes: *Resources.*

Healing: The divine enablement to be God's means for restoring people to wholeness. Contributes: *Wholeness.*

Helps: The divine enablement to attach spiritual value to the accomplishment of practical and necessary tasks that free up, support, and meet the needs of others. Contributes: *Support.*

Hospitality: The divine enablement to care for people by providing fellowship, food, and shelter. Contributes: *Acceptance.*

Intercession: The divine enablement to consistently pray on behalf of and for others, seeing frequent and specific results. Contributes: *Protection.*

Interpretation: The divine enablement to make known to the body of Christ the message of one who is speaking in tongues. Contributes: *Understanding.*

Knowledge: The divine enablement to bring truth to the body through a revelation or biblical insight. Contributes: *Awareness.*

Leadership: The divine enablement to cast vision and to motivate and influence people to harmoniously accomplish the purposes of God. Contributes: *Direction.*

Mercy: The divine enablement to cheerfully and practically help those who are suffering or are in need, having compassion that is moved to action. Contributes: *Care.*

Miracles: The divine enablement to authenticate the ministry and message of God through supernatural interventions that glorify him. Contributes: *God's Power.*

Prophecy: The divine enablement to reveal truth and proclaim it in a timely and relevant manner for understanding, correction, repentance, or edification. Contributes: *Conviction.*

Shepherding: The divine enablement to nurture, care for, and guide people toward ongoing spiritual maturity and becoming like Christ. Contributes: *Nurture.*

Teaching: The divine enablement to understand, clearly explain, and apply the Word of God, causing greater Christlikeness in the lives of listeners. Contributes: *Application.*

Tongues: The divine enablement to receive a spontaneous message from God in public worship and to speak it in an unknown language that is then made known to the church through the gift of interpretation. Contributes: *A Message.*

Wisdom: The divine enablement to effectively apply spiritual truth to meet a need in a specific situation. Contributes: *Guidance.*

resources

Bruce Bugbee has been actively involved with gift-based ministries since 1970. He has provided vision and leadership for churches and individuals seeking to better understand who God has made them to be and how they can make a difference in a meaningful place of service.

In 1986, Bruce coauthored *Network* with Don Cousins and Bill Hybels. It has helped volunteers discover their God-given spiritual gifts, ministry passions, personal style, spiritual maturity, and availability for their rightful place and purpose in the body of Christ through the local church.

Network Ministries International was established in 1993 to serve and support the ministry and mission of the local church in the effective and efficient use of God's people for kingdom purposes. Building up believers, equipping leaders, and establishing harmonious systems mark the impact of Network Ministries International.

Here is a partial list of materials from Network Ministries International to assist you in the identification, placement, and equipping of enthusiastic and gifted leaders and servers in your church. Visit our website at:

www.networkministries.com
or contact our offices directly at (800) 588-8833.

Network Ministry Materials

- Network Kit (includes the following ... and each is available separately)

  Leader's Guide, Participant's Guide, DVD Vignettes (6), PowerPoint™ Presentation, Coach's Guide , User's Guide

- *What You Do Best in the Body of Christ,* Revised and Expanded

  This new edition includes questions for reflection at the end of each chapter and assessments for your spiritual gifts, personal style and ministry passion. Ideal for small groups, Sunday School and individuals. Great resource for new members. Give your leadership teams a vision for the Network process.

- *Discover Your Spiritual Gifts the Network Way* (NEW)

  Now you can discover your spiritual gifts with the best resources available. Includes four gift assessments (experiences, traits, convictions, and observations) plus a ministry assessment!

- *The Gift Book*

  This resource contains an in-depth study of each of the spiritual gifts. Once you have identified your gift ... you can now study and learn how to develop it. (Available late 2005)

- Leadership C.A.R.E.™

  Equipping churches requires equippers! Walk your ministry leaders through the process ... from being primarily program planners and event coordinators ... to leading gift-based ministry teams as people equippers.

  Leader's Guide, PowerPoint™ and a Ministry Leader's Workbook

- The Network Centeronline™ Database

  A database for volunteer placement and ministry management. Keep in touch with all your people resources through the "net" ... the Network Center*online* database. A ready-to-use people-flow tracking system that helps you keep track of all the spiritual gifts, styles, and ministry passions of your servers. Store and sort through all your ministry position descriptions too! Try it free on the Demo Site:

  www.networkcenteronline.com

  (ID=9 Password=serve)

- Leadership Retreats and Onsite Training

  Bring the vision and expertise you need to your church. Bruce Bugbee will work with your staff, church leaders, and congregation. Schedule an event, retreat, or consultation. He brings biblical teaching, passion for the church, leadership understanding, and practical truth with humor and over thirty years of gift-based ministry experience.

Contact
Network Ministries International
for
vision casting/ministry implementation/equipping leaders
www.networkministries.com 800.588.8833

Church Discounts Available!

observation assessment forms

observation
assessment 1

I'd like your opinion!

I am seeking to better understand how God has equipped me to serve others. One part of the process involves getting feedback from a few people who know me reasonably well. Your thoughts about what I do best and the way I relate to others will be very helpful. Please take a few minutes to complete this assessment.

My name is: _____

These are my observations of: _____

Directions:

1. Using the following scale, mark each description according to how true it is of the person you are describing:

Score		Meaning
3	=	Consistently / Definitely true
2	=	Most of the time / Usually true
1	=	Some of the time / Once in a while
0	=	Not at all / Don't know / Haven't observed

2. Circle your score for each description in the appropriately numbered box on pages 2–5.

3. *Important:*

   - Answer according to what seems to be true of the person most of the time, not what you would like them to be or think they should be.
   - If you have seen this person involved and serving in a ministry, then describe your observations in that context. If you have not, then use the observations you have had.

- To what degree do these statements reflect this person's tendencies and behaviors?
- Return the assessment as soon as you have completed it. Thanks!

		Consistently/ Definitely True	Most of the Time/ Usually True	Some of the Time/ Once in a While	Don't Know/ Haven't Observed	
A	Develops strategies or plans to reach identified goals; organizes people, tasks, and events; helps organizations or groups become more efficient; creates order out of organizational chaos.	3	2	1	0	
B	Works creatively with wood, cloth, metal, paints, glass, etc.; works with different kinds of tools; makes things for practical uses; designs and builds things; works with his or her hands.	3	2	1	0	
C	Communicates with variety and creativity; develops and uses particular artistic skills (art, drama, music, photography, etc.); finds new and fresh ways to communicate ideas to others.	3	2	1	0	
D	Strengthens and reassures troubled people; encourages or challenges them; motivates others to grow; supports those who seem to be stuck and need to take action.	3	2	1	0	
E	Trusts God to answer prayer and encourages others to do the same; has confidence in God's continuing presence and ability to help, even in difficult times; moves forward in spite of difficulties or opposition.	3	2	1	0	
F	Gives liberally and joyfully to people in financial need; gives generously to projects requiring substantial support; manages his or her money well in order to free more of it for other people and causes.	3	2	1	0	
G	Works behind the scenes to support the work of others; finds small things that need to be done and does them without being asked; helps wherever needed, even with routine or mundane tasks.	3	2	1	0	

		Consistently/ Definitely True	Most of the Time/ Usually True	Some of the Time/ Once in a While	Don't Know/ Haven't Observed	
H	Meets new people and helps them to feel welcome; entertains guests; opens his or her home to others who need a safe, supportive environment; puts people at ease in unfamiliar surroundings.	3	2	1	0	
I	Continually offers to pray for others; has confidence in the Lord's protection; spends a lot of time praying; is convinced that God moves in direct response to prayer.	3	2	1	0	
J	Takes responsibility for directing groups; motivates and guides others to reach important goals; manages people and resources well; influences others to perform to the best of their abilities.	3	2	1	0	
K	Empathizes with hurting people; patiently and compassionately walks with people through painful experiences; helps those generally regarded as undeserving or beyond help.	3	2	1	0	
L	Pioneers new undertakings (such as a new church or ministry); serves in another country or community; adapts to different cultures and surroundings; demonstrates cultural awareness and sensitivity.	3	2	1	0	
M	Speaks with conviction to bring change in the lives of others; exposes cultural trends, teaching, or events that are morally wrong or harmful; boldly speaks truth even in places where it may be unpopular.	3	2	1	0	
N	Looks for opportunities to build relationships with unbelievers; communicates openly and effectively about his or her faith; talks about spiritual matters with those who don't believe.	3	2	1	0	
O	Faithfully provides long-term support and nurture for a group of people; provides guidance for the whole person; patiently but firmly nurtures others in their development as believers.	3	2	1	0	

		Consistently/ Definitely True	Most of the Time/ Usually True	Some of the Time/ Once in a While	Don't Know/ Haven't Observed	
P	Studies, understands, and communicates biblical truth; develops appropriate teaching material and presents it effectively; communicates in ways that motivate others to change.	3	2	1	0	
Q	Distinguishes between truth and error, good and evil; accurately judges character; sees through phoniness and deceit; helps others to see rightness or wrongness in life situations.	3	2	1	0	
R	Carefully studies and researches subjects he or she wants to understand better; shares his or her knowledge and insights with others when asked; sometimes gains information that is not attained by natural observation or means.	3	2	1	0	
S	Sees simple, practical solutions in the midst of conflict or confusion; gives helpful advice to others facing complicated life situations; helps people take practical action to solve real problems.	3	2	1	0	
T	Demonstrates the power of God by bringing restoration to the sick and diseased by laying hands on them and praying; miraculously heals a person's body, soul, or spirit.	3	2	1	0	
U	Communicates God's message to others when someone speaks in tongues; responds to people who have spoken in a different and unknown language and tells the group what God is saying.	3	2	1	0	
V	Speaks God's truth and has it authenticated by an accompanying miracle; communicates the ministry and message of Jesus Christ with demonstrations of power over nature and claims God to be the source of the miracle.	3	2	1	0	
W	Speaks in a language I do not understand, and when she or he does, someone speaks out to interpret what they just said; worships God and seems to spontaneously pray using words I have not heard before.	3	2	1	0	

Here are a few additional questions:

	Top Three Letters
1. Go back over those you marked with a "3" (Consistently / Definitely True) and in the shaded column, indicate your top choice with a 1, second with a 2, and third with a 3. Then write the "letter" of those top three in the space provided to the right.	1. _____ 2. _____ 3. _____
2. If you are familiar with spiritual gifts, which one(s) have you seen most in this person's life?	1. _____ 2. _____ 3. _____
3. Are there any other observations or insights you have that would help this person better understand what they do best?	Comments

Thank you for taking the time to complete this assessment. Your opinions and observations are valuable to me. I appreciate your help!

observation
assessment 2

I'd like your opinion!

I am seeking to better understand how God has equipped me to serve others. One part of the process involves getting feedback from a few people who know me reasonably well. Your thoughts about what I do best and the way I relate to others will be very helpful. Please take a few minutes to complete this assessment.

My name is: _____

These are my observations of: _____

Directions:

1. Using the following scale, mark each description according to how true it is of the person you are describing:

Score		Meaning
3	=	Consistently / Definitely true
2	=	Most of the time / Usually true
1	=	Some of the time / Once in a while
0	=	Not at all / Don't know / Haven't observed

2. Circle your score for each description in the appropriately numbered box on pages 2–5.

3. *Important:*

   * Answer according to what seems to be true of the person most of the time, not what you would like them to be or think they should be.
   * If you have seen this person involved and serving in a ministry, then describe your observations in that context. If you have not, then use the observations you have had.

- To what degree do these statements reflect this person's tendencies and behaviors?
- Return the assessment as soon as you have completed it. Thanks!

		Consistently/ Definitely True	Most of the Time/ Usually True	Some of the Time/ Once in a While	Don't Know/ Haven't Observed	
A	Develops strategies or plans to reach identified goals; organizes people, tasks, and events; helps organizations or groups become more efficient; creates order out of organizational chaos.	3	2	1	0	
B	Works creatively with wood, cloth, metal, paints, glass, etc.; works with different kinds of tools; makes things for practical uses; designs and builds things; works with his or her hands.	3	2	1	0	
C	Communicates with variety and creativity; develops and uses particular artistic skills (art, drama, music, photography, etc.); finds new and fresh ways to communicate ideas to others.	3	2	1	0	
D	Strengthens and reassures troubled people; encourages or challenges them; motivates others to grow; supports those who seem to be stuck and need to take action.	3	2	1	0	
E	Trusts God to answer prayer and encourages others to do the same; has confidence in God's continuing presence and ability to help, even in difficult times; moves forward in spite of difficulties or opposition.	3	2	1	0	
F	Gives liberally and joyfully to people in financial need; gives generously to projects requiring substantial support; manages his or her money well in order to free more of it for other people and causes.	3	2	1	0	
G	Works behind the scenes to support the work of others; finds small things that need to be done and does them without being asked; helps wherever needed, even with routine or mundane tasks.	3	2	1	0	

		Consistently/ Definitely True	Most of the Time/ Usually True	Some of the Time/ Once in a While	Don't Know/ Haven't Observed
H	Meets new people and helps them to feel welcome; entertains guests; opens his or her home to others who need a safe, supportive environment; puts people at ease in unfamiliar surroundings.	3	2	1	0
I	Continually offers to pray for others; has confidence in the Lord's protection; spends a lot of time praying; is convinced that God moves in direct response to prayer.	3	2	1	0
J	Takes responsibility for directing groups; motivates and guides others to reach important goals; manages people and resources well; influences others to perform to the best of their abilities.	3	2	1	0
K	Empathizes with hurting people; patiently and compassionately walks with people through painful experiences; helps those generally regarded as undeserving or beyond help	3	2	1	0
L	Pioneers new undertakings (such as a new church or ministry); serves in another country or community; adapts to different cultures and surroundings; demonstrates cultural awareness and sensitivity.	3	2	1	0
M	Speaks with conviction to bring change in the lives of others; exposes cultural trends, teaching, or events that are morally wrong or harmful; boldly speaks truth even in places where it may be unpopular.	3	2	1	0
N	Looks for opportunities to build relationships with unbelievers; communicates openly and effectively about his or her faith; talks about spiritual matters with those who don't believe.	3	2	1	0
O	Faithfully provides long-term support and nurture for a group of people; provides guidance for the whole person; patiently but firmly nurtures others in their development as believers.	3	2	1	0

		Consistently/ Definitely True	Most of the Time/ Usually True	Some of the Time/ Once in a While	Don't Know/ Haven't Observed	
P	Studies, understands, and communicates biblical truth; develops appropriate teaching material and presents it effectively; communicates in ways that motivate others to change.	3	2	1	0	
Q	Distinguishes between truth and error, good and evil; accurately judges character; sees through phoniness and deceit; helps others to see rightness or wrongness in life situations.	3	2	1	0	
R	Carefully studies and researches subjects he or she wants to understand better; shares his or her knowledge and insights with others when asked; sometimes gains information that is not attained by natural observation or means.	3	2	1	0	
S	Sees simple, practical solutions in the midst of conflict or confusion; gives helpful advice to others facing complicated life situations; helps people take practical action to solve real problems.	3	2	1	0	
T	Demonstrates the power of God by bringing restoration to the sick and diseased by laying hands on them and praying; miraculously heals a person's body, soul, or spirit.	3	2	1	0	
U	Communicates God's message to others when someone speaks in tongues; responds to people who have spoken in a different and unknown language and tells the group what God is saying.	3	2	1	0	
V	Speaks God's truth and has it authenticated by an accompanying miracle; communicates the ministry and message of Jesus Christ with demonstrations of power over nature and claims God to be the source of the miracle.	3	2	1	0	
W	Speaks in a language I do not understand, and when she or he does, someone speaks out to interpret what they just said; worships God and seems to spontaneously pray using words I have not heard before.	3	2	1	0	

Here are a few additional questions:

1. Go back over those you marked with a "3" (Consistently / Definitely True) and in the shaded column, indicate your top choice with a 1, second with a 2, and third with a 3. Then write the "letter" of those top three in the space provided to the right.	Top Three Letters 1. _____ 2. _____ 3. _____
2. If you are familiar with spiritual gifts, which one(s) have you seen most in this person's life?	1. _____ 2. _____ 3. _____
3. Are there any other observations or insights you have that would help this person better understand what they do best?	Comments

Thank you for taking the time to complete this assessment. Your opinions and observations are valuable to me. I appreciate your help!

observation assessment 3

I'd like your opinion!

I am seeking to better understand how God has equipped me to serve others. One part of the process involves getting feedback from a few people who know me reasonably well. Your thoughts about what I do best and the way I relate to others will be very helpful. Please take a few minutes to complete this assessment.

My name is: _____

These are my observations of: _____

Directions:

1. Using the following scale, mark each description according to how true it is of the person you are describing:

Score		Meaning
3	=	Consistently / Definitely true
2	=	Most of the time / Usually true
1	=	Some of the time / Once in a while
0	=	Not at all / Don't know / Haven't observed

2. Circle your score for each description in the appropriately numbered box on pages 2–5.

3. *Important:*

   * Answer according to what seems to be true of the person most of the time, not what you would like them to be or think they should be.
   * If you have seen this person involved and serving in a ministry, then describe your observations in that context. If you have not, then use the observations you have had.

- To what degree do these statements reflect this person's tendencies and behaviors?
- Return the assessment as soon as you have completed it. Thanks!

		Consistently/ Definitely True	Most of the Time/ Usually True	Some of the Time/ Once in a While	Don't Know/ Haven't Observed	
A	Develops strategies or plans to reach identified goals; organizes people, tasks, and events; helps organizations or groups become more efficient; creates order out of organizational chaos.	3	2	1	0	
B	Works creatively with wood, cloth, metal, paints, glass, etc.; works with different kinds of tools; makes things for practical uses; designs and builds things; works with his or her hands.	3	2	1	0	
C	Communicates with variety and creativity; develops and uses particular artistic skills (art, drama, music, photography, etc.); finds new and fresh ways to communicate ideas to others.	3	2	1	0	
D	Strengthens and reassures troubled people; encourages or challenges them; motivates others to grow; supports those who seem to be stuck and need to take action.	3	2	1	0	
E	Trusts God to answer prayer and encourages others to do the same; has confidence in God's continuing presence and ability to help, even in difficult times; moves forward in spite of difficulties or opposition.	3	2	1	0	
F	Gives liberally and joyfully to people in financial need; gives generously to projects requiring substantial support; manages his or her money well in order to free more of it for other people and causes.	3	2	1	0	
G	Works behind the scenes to support the work of others; finds small things that need to be done and does them without being asked; helps wherever needed, even with routine or mundane tasks.	3	2	1	0	

		Consistently/ Definitely True	Most of the Time/ Usually True	Some of the Time/ Once in a While	Don't Know/ Haven't Observed	
H	Meets new people and helps them to feel welcome; entertains guests; opens his or her home to others who need a safe, supportive environment; puts people at ease in unfamiliar surroundings.	3	2	1	0	
I	Continually offers to pray for others; has confidence in the Lord's protection; spends a lot of time praying; is convinced that God moves in direct response to prayer.	3	2	1	0	
J	Takes responsibility for directing groups; motivates and guides others to reach important goals; manages people and resources well; influences others to perform to the best of their abilities.	3	2	1	0	
K	Empathizes with hurting people; patiently and compassionately walks with people through painful experiences; helps those generally regarded as undeserving or beyond help.	3	2	1	0	
L	Pioneers new undertakings (such as a new church or ministry); serves in another country or community; adapts to different cultures and surroundings; demonstrates cultural awareness and sensitivity.	3	2	1	0	
M	Speaks with conviction to bring change in the lives of others; exposes cultural trends, teaching, or events that are morally wrong or harmful; boldly speaks truth even in places where it may be unpopular.	3	2	1	0	
N	Looks for opportunities to build relationships with unbelievers; communicates openly and effectively about his or her faith; talks about spiritual matters with those who don't believe.	3	2	1	0	
O	Faithfully provides long-term support and nurture for a group of people; provides guidance for the whole person; patiently but firmly nurtures others in their development as believers.	3	2	1	0	

		Consistently/ Definitely True	Most of the Time/ Usually True	Some of the Time/ Once in a While	Don't Know/ Haven't Observed
P	Studies, understands, and communicates biblical truth; develops appropriate teaching material and presents it effectively; communicates in ways that motivate others to change.	3	2	1	0
Q	Distinguishes between truth and error, good and evil; accurately judges character; sees through phoniness and deceit; helps others to see rightness or wrongness in life situations.	3	2	1	0
R	Carefully studies and researches subjects he or she wants to understand better; shares his or her knowledge and insights with others when asked; sometimes gains information that is not attained by natural observation or means.	3	2	1	0
S	Sees simple, practical solutions in the midst of conflict or confusion; gives helpful advice to others facing complicated life situations; helps people take practical action to solve real problems.	3	2	1	0
T	Demonstrates the power of God by bringing restoration to the sick and diseased by laying hands on them and praying; miraculously heals a person's body, soul, or spirit.	3	2	1	0
U	Communicates God's message to others when someone speaks in tongues; responds to people who have spoken in a different and unknown language and tells the group what God is saying.	3	2	1	0
V	Speaks God's truth and has it authenticated by an accompanying miracle; communicates the ministry and message of Jesus Christ with demonstrations of power over nature and claims God to be the source of the miracle.	3	2	1	0
W	Speaks in a language I do not understand, and when she or he does, someone speaks out to interpret what they just said; worships God and seems to spontaneously pray using words I have not heard before.	3	2	1	0

Here are a few additional questions:

1. Go back over those you marked with a "3" (Consistently / Definitely True) and in the shaded column, indicate your top choice with a 1, second with a 2, and third with a 3. Then write the "letter" of those top three in the space provided to the right.	Top Three Letters 1. _____ 2. _____ 3. _____
2. If you are familiar with spiritual gifts, which one(s) have you seen most in this person's life?	1. _____ 2. _____ 3. _____
3. Are there any other observations or insights you have that would help this person better understand what they do best?	Comments

Thank you for taking the time to complete this assessment. Your opinions and observations are valuable to me. I appreciate your help!

WILLOW
Willow Creek Association

Willow Creek Association
Vision, Training, Resources for Prevailing Churches

This resource was created to serve you and to help you build a local church that prevails. It is just one of many ministry tools that are part of the Willow Creek Resources® line, published by the Willow Creek Association together with Zondervan.

The Willow Creek Association (WCA) was created in 1992 to serve a rapidly growing number of churches from across the denominational spectrum that are committed to helping unchurched people become fully devoted followers of Christ. Membership in the WCA now numbers over 10,000 Member Churches worldwide from more than ninety denominations.

The Willow Creek Association links like-minded Christian leaders with each other and with strategic vision, training, and resources in order to help them build prevailing churches designed to reach their redemptive potential. Here are some of the ways the WCA does that.

- **Prevailing Church Conference**—an annual two-and-a-half day event, held at Willow Creek Community Church in South Barrington, Illinois, to help pioneering church leaders raise up a volunteer core while discovering new and innovative ways to build prevailing churches that reach unchurched people.

- **Leadership Summit**—a once-a-year, two-and-a-half-day conference to envision and equip Christians with leadership gifts and responsibilities. Presented live at Willow Creek as well as via satellite broadcast to over sixty locations across North America, this event is designed to increase the leadership effectiveness of pastors, ministry staff, volunteer church leaders, and Christians in the marketplace.

- **Ministry-Specific Conferences**—throughout each year the WCA hosts a variety of conferences and training events—both at Willow Creek's main campus and offsite, across the U.S. and around the world—targeting church leaders in ministry-specific areas such as: evangelism, the arts, children, students, small groups, preaching and teaching, spiritual formation, spiritual gifts, raising up resources, etc.

- **Willow Creek Resources®**—to provide churches with trusted and field-tested ministry resources in such areas as leadership, evangelism, spiritual formation, spiritual gifts, small groups, stewardship, student ministry, children's ministry, the use of the arts—drama, media, contemporary music—and more. For additional information about Willow Creek Resources® call the Customer Service Center at 800-570-9812. Outside the U.S. call 847-765-0070.

- *WillowNet*—the WCA's Internet resource service, which provides access to hundreds of transcripts of Willow Creek messages, drama scripts, songs, videos, and multimedia tools. The system allows users to sort through these elements and download them for a fee. Visit us online at www.willowcreek.com.

- **WCA News**—a quarterly publication to inform you of the latest trends, resources, and information on WCA events from around the world.

- *Defining Moments*—a monthly audio journal for church leaders featuring Bill Hybels and other Christian leaders discussing probing issues to help you discover biblical principles and transferable strategies to maximize your church's redemptive potential.

- *The Exchange*—our online classified ads service to assist churches in recruiting key staff for ministry positions.

- **Member Benefits**—includes substantial discounts to WCA training events, a 20 percent discount on all Willow Creek Resources®, access to a Members-Only section on WillowNet, monthly communications, and more. Member Churches also receive special discounts and premier services through WCA's growing number of ministry partners—Select Service Providers.

For specific information about WCA membership, upcoming conferences, and other ministry services contact:

Willow Creek Association
P.O. Box 3188, Barrington, IL 60011-3188
Phone: 847-570-9812
Fax: 847-765-5046
www.willowcreek.com

Network Revised

The Right People, in the Right Places, for the Right Reasons, at the Right Time

Bruce L. Bugbee, Don Cousins, Bill Hybels

Network Revised is a six-session dynamic program to help Christians understand who God has uniquely made them to be and to mobilize them to a place of meaningful service in the local church. Each participant in *Network Revised* will work through a series of assessments which leads them to discover their unique blend of spiritual gifts, personal style, and ministry passion. The participants are also taught the biblical nature and purpose of the church as the body of Christ and the unique importance of each member's contribution. The *Network Revised* material was developed by Bruce Bugbee, Don Cousins, and Bill Hybels of Willow Creek Community Church to motivate people to discover, connect, and apply their unique blend of passion, gifts, and style to specific ministry opportunities. Over 800,000 people have gone through *Network Revised*.

Network Revised works with any size group, from small groups of 4–12 to large groups of 15 to 150 or more. *Network Revised* can be presented successfully in these different formats: 1. Three sessions of two hours each 2. Six sessions of 50 minutes each 3. One-, two-, or three-day retreats 4. The one that works best for your church!

Summary of revisions:
- Now six sessions
- Revisions allow for more complete self-understanding (Servant Profile) and ministry placement.
- Session on passion now includes a list of "Passion Categories" for easier identification and database retrieval
- Revised video vignettes (4) include ethnic diversity
- DVD segment for each of the six sessions
- Overheads reformatted, creating a PowerPoint presentation for the six sessions on a CD-ROM
- User's Guide and Consultant's Guide now on CD-ROM

The *Network Revised* Kit includes:
- Leader's Guide
- Participant's Guide
- DVD with drama vignettes, vision and coaching material
- CD-ROM includes PowerPoint materials for leaders, users, and consultants, as well as 400 ministry position descriptions

Curriculum Kit: 0-310-25793-X
Leader's Guide: 0-310-25794-8
Participant's Guide: 0-310-25795-6
DVD: 0-310-25796-4
PowerPoint® CD: 0-310-25797-2

Look for Network Revised *at your favorite bookstore!*

What You Do Best in the Body of Christ

Discover Your Spiritual Gifts, Personal Style, and God-Given Passion

Bruce L. Bugbee

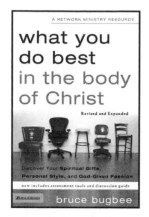

Have you found fulfillment in life? Can you say your ministry is a fruitful one? God has created you to be both fulfilled and fruitful in a meaningful place of ministry. You can discover your God-given design and the role he created for you in and through the local church. In *What You Do Best*, Bruce Bugbee helps you identify your God-given passion, spiritual gifts, and personal style. And he shows how together they point to your unique role and purpose in the body of Christ. Drawing from biblical principles, *What You Do Best* provides proven tools and a conversational approach that will guide you to a greater fulfillment of God's will for your life. You'll discover: Your God-given passion indicates where you should serve—Your God-given spiritual gifts indicate what you should do—Your God-given personal style indicates how you should serve. Together, they indicate what you do best. You'll find plenty of helpful charts and self-assessments, plus insights into the fallacies and pitfalls that can hinder your effectiveness. "You are needed in the church," says Bruce Bugbee, "not because there are slots to fill, but because in and through your ministry, God's grace is released and his purposes are fulfilled." Start learning today what God wants you to do, and experience more enthusiasm, greater joy, and real significance in your life and ministry.

This expanded edition includes discussion questions and fills the need for small groups who are unable, or whose church is unwilling, to implement the value of gifts-based ministry throughout the church.

Softcover: 0-310-25735-2

Pick up a copy today at your favorite bookstore!

ZONDERVAN™

GRAND RAPIDS, MICHIGAN 49530 USA

WWW.ZONDERVAN.COM

WILLOW

Willow Creek Resources

We want to hear from you. Please send your comments about this
book to us in care of zreview@zondervan.com. Thank you.

GRAND RAPIDS, MICHIGAN 49530 USA

WWW.ZONDERVAN.COM